# CREATIVE NATURE CRAFTS

# CREATIVE
# NATURE
# CRAFTS

*Use Nature's bounty to make beautiful
gifts and decorations*

ALISON JENKINS
WITH TEXT BY TESSA EVELEGH

COURAGE
BOOKS

AN IMPRINT OF RUNNING PRESS
PHILADELPHIA • LONDON

A QUINTET BOOK

Canadian Representatives:
General Publishing Co., Ltd.
30 Lesmill Road, Don Mills
Ontario M3B 2T6

9 8 7 6 5 4 3 2 1

Digit on the right indicates the number of this printing

Library of Congress
Cataloging-in-Publication Number
94-72714

ISBN 1-56138-572-7

This book was designed and produced by
Quintet Publishing Limited
6 Blundell Street
London N7 9BH

Creative Director: Richard Dewing
Designer: Isobel Gillan
Project Editor: Helen Denholm
Editor: Sue Thraves
Photographer: Paul Forrester

Typeset in Great Britain by
Central Southern Typesetters, Eastbourne
Manufacted in Singapore by Bright Arts Pte. Ltd.
Printed in Singapore by Star Standard Pte. Ltd.

Published by Courage Books
an imprint of Running Press Book Publishers
125 South Twenty-second Street
Philadelphia, Pennsylvania 19103-4399

# Contents

# introduction

Since time began, mankind has known that nature is the best designer. The subtlety of natural colors and the astonishing variety of forms can never quite be matched by anything we could ever dream up. And, traditionally, we have delighted in taking nature's bounty to use in making things for ourselves to decorate our homes and surroundings, and to make into gifts. Particularly during festivals and at times of celebration, cultures the world over have looked to nature to provide the decoration, gleaning a little of what she has and gathering it together to make striking seasonal displays.

The appeal of using natural materials is that you are immediately bestowed with an exquisite color scheme that is at one with the surroundings, and by working with the seasons, you are continually being presented with new materials that provide an ever-revolving cycle of different textures and forms. By the same season next year, your ideas will have developed, even if by just the slightest amount, and the gifts and decorations you make will have a fresh, new look. Before you know it, you will be part of an ancient tradition of folk art, in which traditional crafts become part of the culture's visual vocabulary. And, like language itself, folk art is continually developing.

The appeal of creative nature crafts is that you don't have to be a great artist or hugely innovative to produce gifts and decorations of great beauty. You just need a love for all things natural, and the knowledge that anything you make with them will take on nature's own beauty. At the same time, take a lesson from the apprentice craftspeople of a bygone age: they didn't expect perfect results at their very first attempt – the joy was the mastering of a skill and developing their own signature. Most of the ideas in this book require no particular skill, but some techniques do take a little practice to get right. So give yourself time to master the art, and remember that it is during the learning process that many artists and craftspeople have discovered their own particular technique and style. If you don't like something, have the courage to recycle or scrap it and to start again. Very often the simplest ideas work best, so don't try to be ambitious – a pressed flower collage need be no more than one bloom or a line of leaves. As you become more confident of

working with a particular material, learning its strengths and limitations, you will find you develop an instinct for what works well.

The start of every decoration or gift has to be the collection of the necessary materials – and in many cases, the preservation of them too. And although the countryside has plenty of beautiful things to offer, nobody who loves nature would want to be responsible for plundering it. Many countries prohibit the removal of certain endangered species, and some even outlaw removing anything from their coastlines. It's best to ask about the local regulations in each area when traveling.

Much of the materials used in this book can be gleaned from gardens, but if you are also adding treasures from the hedgerows, make sure that your clipping would hardly be noticed, leaving enough behind to let nature replenish herself in the wild.

# Spring

♥

A season of contrasts, spring enters as the first quiet shoots appear on a bare landscape, and departs with an explosion of color and new life. Since time began, this astonishing display has prompted man to celebrate. So enjoy the abundance – there's plenty around for us to gather for decorating our homes without diminishing nature's own display outside.

Spring is a season of high drama. It arrives quietly enough, with delicate snowdrops pushing through frosted earth, and blossom buds fattening on the unpromising bare branches of fruit trees. Yet with the encouragement of just a few warmer days, nature puts on her very best show. Delicate leaves in brilliant emeralds clad the trees like translucent skirts, while still letting the form of the branches show through. On the ground, bulbs burst forth at an astonishing rate, throwing a coverlet of vivid shades over the countryside. This is the time of the year when flowers appear in the purest of colors – rich yellows, sapphire blues, and clear scarlets, shining out in almost neon shades as if to herald the bright hope of warmer days to come, even if the weather is still sometimes decidedly inclement. Many, like daffodils, tulips, and hyacinths, come in simple, robust forms that look as if they can withstand the worst of spring gusts and gales. Others, like snowdrops, primroses, and crocuses, look improbably delicate, yet bravely withstand the worst of the weather to decorate the countryside in the early months of the year. In centuries past, these tiny flowers, which heralded the end of winter, brought hope

indeed. Soon, the dwindling food supplies would be replenished, and the bleak, cold days and long dark nights would be just a memory. The countryside would become richly attired in the vibrant shades of spring. This astonishing show of rebirth, giving hope of easier days to come, has touched the heart of man since the very origins of civilization, and he has marked it with celebration. Now is the time to collect twigs and new shoots, and to gather flowers from the countryside and turn them into gifts.

## SPRING CELEBRATIONS

The exuberance of new life seems to prompt us into one long celebration in spring – but as if to stop us from getting too carried away, this is punctuated in the Christian calendar by a period of forty days' fasting during Lent. Valentine's Day comes first, on February 14, right at the very dawn of spring. This is the time when hopeful young men and women anonymously exchange gifts and cards in a declaration of love. The custom dates back to the Roman festival of Lupercalia, during which they performed fertility rites in honor of Juno, the goddess of women and marriage.

The Christian church named this festival after Saint Valentine, who was executed in A.D. 270 for marrying young soldiers. Such weddings were forbidden by the Emperor Claudius as he felt love would diminish their fighting spirit.

The forty days' abstinence of Lent comes soon after Valentine's Day – to be relieved only on the fourth Sunday by Mothering Sunday in Britain, when mothers are traditionally presented with a posy of flowers by their children. In America Mother's Day is celebrated on the second Sunday in May.

Finally, Easter arrives, to mark the full maturity of spring. It's a movable feast (the timing is worked out according to the moon's phases), which can fall anywhere between March 22 and April 25. Easter has its roots in pagan times, when an ancient festival was celebrated in honor of Eastre, the Anglo-Saxon goddess of spring and fertility. The modern Christian festival celebrates Jesus rising from the dead, symbolically offering everlasting life to mankind. It is no accident that this coincides with the Jewish Passover as Jesus' Last Supper was a Passover meal celebrating the Exodus from Egypt, which offered the Jews a new beginning.

By Easter, spring is at its height, offering the full diversity of what nature has to offer. The blooms are at their fullest and lushest before they die down to make way for the shades and forms of summer. The abundance makes for rich pickings from gardens and hedgerows, while also providing for plentiful cheap blooms in the marketplace. Homes can be decked generously with what nature has to offer, yet plenty can be left still growing outside.

## DECORATED EGGS

Symbolic of new life and the resurrection, eggs have been colored and decorated for centuries. Just the addition of colored eggs to spring flowers turns a fresh arrangement into an Easter decoration. Gather spring flowers *en masse* into a simple vase, then place a container of eggs next to this to make an instant Easter centerpiece. They could be nestled in moss in a wire or wicker basket, laid in a cool enamel bowl, or tucked into a small nest (available from florists). Eggs can be colored using special edible dye or regular food colorings if they are going to be eaten. If they're to be used purely for decoration, you can use fabric dyes, which can create fabulous rainbow effects. Natural dyes can be used too: the traditional one is onion skin dye, which creates a wonderful coppery glow; another effective and easy-to-get-hold-of coloring is turmeric. Alternatively, you can use natural dyes that are generally used for fabrics. The charm of coloring your own eggs is that the natural defects in the shell mean there are subtle gradations of color, speckles, and marble-like veins. If you plan to blow the eggs, do so after you have dyed them; otherwise you will have to weight the eggs down to stop them floating to the top of the liquid. Whatever kind of coloring you use, you'll notice it becomes less effective the more eggs you do, which you can use to your advantage to make eggs in subtly gradated colors.

## ONION SKIN DYE

Peel about six onions, and put the skins in a large pan filled with enough water to cover six eggs. Add six tablespoons of salt and two of vinegar to fix the color, and boil until you are satisfied with the color of the eggshells. Lift out with a wooden spoon, and let dry on paper towels.

## USING FOOD COLORING

Empty a small bottle of food coloring into about 1¼ cups of water and add two table-spoons of vinegar.

## USING FABRIC DYE

Make up the dye in preserve jars. Add about half a disk of dye to the jar, pour on 1¼ cups of hot water, and add two tablespoons of vinegar. Using a wooden spoon, lower in one or two eggs depending on the size of the jar, and leave until they have achieved the desired shade. This can take up to half an hour.

## TO DECORATE THE EGGS

Once you've mastered the knack of dyeing eggs, it can be fun to decorate them. One of the simplest ways is to engrave them using a sharp craft knife. This is a tradition that goes back centuries in Europe, when young girls would scratch motifs of plants, animals, and hearts onto colored eggshells. First, dye the eggs; when they are completely dry, you can start to engrave. It's best to work using plenty of short strokes, going over lines you've already scratched until you have achieved the thickness of line you require. It is easier to work directly onto the eggshell, rather than trying to pencil in a design, which may leave marks and smudges. One of the easiest ways to insure a well-spaced design is to scratch lines around the egg first to divide it into quarters, then you have only a small motif to engrave into each quarter. Alternatively, engrave a message or even the name of the recipient.

Another way to decorate eggs is to use leaves and flowers to make imprints on eggshells. Choose those with the flattest surface that will closely hug the egg's surface, then tie on a piece of nylon pantyhose to hold them in position. Lower the egg into the dye, and leave it until it has achieved the desired color. You can either put the leaves onto the plain eggshell, or create two-color effects by first quickly dyeing the egg to give a pale shade, letting it dry, then applying a leaf or flower and redyeing. It all takes a bit of practice, so don't feel despondent if your first attempts are not brilliant. These simple forms of egg decoration are a delight to do as you can never be exactly sure of the outcome. There's always the anticipation of what the effect will be as you lift the eggs out of the dye, or cut off the nylon to reveal anything from perfect imprints to delicate marbled or veined effects.

## USING BRANCHES AND TWIGS

In Continental Europe sprouting branches of fruit trees are traditionally used to make Easter trees. They are cut when the buds are being formed, put into large jugs of water, and decorated with small wooden eggs. As Easter approaches, the branches gradually become covered with delicate blossoms. Some of the evergreens are effective too – larch, with its tiny pinecones from the previous year, breaks out in the tiny bright green tufts of this year's needles and crimson tufted flowers. Then there are the endless varieties of trees that produce catkins in delicate shades of silver, pink, and gold. Even if you don't want to plunder the countryside, these are not expensive to buy, and even just three branches can make a dramatic Easter display.

Young twigs are also wonderful and flexible, and can be used to make all kinds of gifts – from decorative hearts to baskets, trays and mats. Cut them as long as you can, and make them up while flexible. The twigs dry out leaving gifts that last.

# Willow Valentine Heart

*Made from young willow branches, this beautiful wall decoration will last through many springtimes. For centuries the heart shape has been a symbol of love and friendship, and it is used extensively as a motif for craft work of all kinds. It was during the 1850s that Valentine's Day assumed a particular significance. Until then, heart-shaped tokens were exchanged throughout the year as tokens of affection.*

## MATERIALS

- 8 to 10 long thin willow twigs
- pair of sharp scissors or pruning shears
- ball of string
- 1 yard ribbon

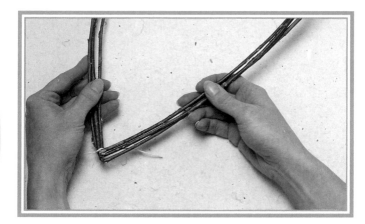

**1** *First soak the willow twigs overnight in water. A bathtub is the best place to do this because they will become soft and pliable. Take three twigs and tie them together at the center with a piece of string. Bend carefully in half.*

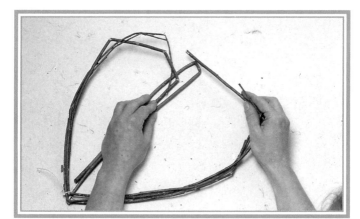

**2** *Bend a 30-inch twig in half to form a hanging loop. Place this at the center, and bend the ends of the first twigs around to meet it. Tie this central bundle together with string.*

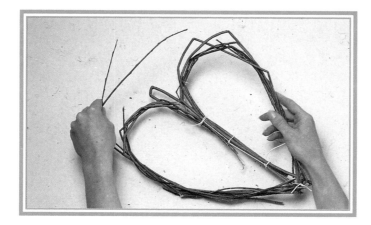

**3** *Wind the remaining twigs loosely around the heart-shaped base, tucking in the ends neatly as you go. If the twigs become dry and brittle, just soak them again in water. Tie a ribbon bow around the center twigs to finish.*

# Decorated Easter Eggs

*Use edible dyes if you're going to eat the eggs, or fabric dyes if they're purely for display. Traditionally representative of fertility and creation, decorated eggs have become an essential part of Easter celebrations. A variety of methods can be employed to transform a simple plain egg into a beautiful keepsake or a colorful prize in an Easter egg hunt. This collection of Easter eggs can be delicately engraved, printed, or simply painted and dyed.*

## MATERIALS

- large eggs
- tablespoon
- selection of food dyes
- salt
- vinegar
- paper towels
- bodkin
- glass bowl or jar
- sharp craft knife
- ball of string
- small leaves or ferns
- old pair of nylon pantyhose or stockings
- large bundle of raffia
- acrylic poster paints
- masking tape

**1** ***For dyed eggs****, make up a solution of 2½ cups of cold water and a bottle of food dye. This makes a strong color, so use less dye if a paler shade is required. Add 1 tablespoon of both salt and vinegar to act as a fixative, and stir well. Lower the egg into the solution, and leave until the color is satisfactory.*

### Note
*Edible eggs should be hard cooked before dyeing. Decorative eggs should be dyed raw and blown when dry.*

**2** **For engraved eggs**, dye a raw egg, and let it dry. Blow the egg by piercing a hole at each end with a bodkin, hold it over a bowl, and blow out the contents. Rinse the empty shell, and let it dry. Use a sharp craft knife and scratch light guidelines onto the egg.

*Continue with a light scratching action to reveal the plain shell color beneath the film of dye.*

**3** **For leaf prints**, place a leaf or small fern on an undyed egg. Cut a square from a pair of pantyhose or stockings, and wrap it tightly around the egg to hold the leaf in place and act as a resist when the egg is dyed. Dye the egg as described in step 1. Remove the egg from the dye, and let it dry before removing the nylon

*mesh; otherwise the dye will bleed onto the resist area and the design will be ruined.*

**For raffia bundles**, take eight strands of raffia approximately 20 inches long. Divide them into two bundles, and tie each at intervals with small pieces of raffia. Fold the two bundles in half, and tie securely at the fold point and at the top.

Blow three eggs, and paint each one a different color using poster or acrylic paints. Insert the eggs into the raffia bundle, holding in place with a little masking tape if necessary.

Thread a bodkin with a strand of raffia. Secure the eggs inside the bundle by taking the strand horizontally around each egg and looping around each vertical group of strands. Finish by tying on a raffia bow.

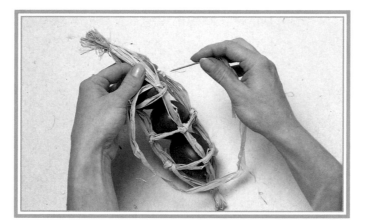

# Springtime Posies

*In the days when opportunities for courtship were restricted, the symbolism of flowers could be used to great effect. Lovers could use flowers to exchange messages and even set up meetings because certain flowers were representative of different times of the day. Conventionally, they consisted of a large central flower, like this rose, surrounded by concentric rings of contrasting flowers and/or herbs.*

MATERIALS

- a selection of fresh flowers
- pair of sharp scissors or pruning shears
- floral tape
- a selection of herbs

**1** *Trim the flower stalks so that they are approximately the same size. Start at the center with a pretty bloom such as a rose. Wind a length of floral tape around its stem, and add four or five other blooms. Wind the tape around to secure the second ring of flowers to the first.*

**2** *Add some aromatic herbs such as sage, rosemary or mint. To complete the posy, add a few sprigs of variegated ivy to signify fidelity, and to increase the volume of the arrangement.*

**3** *Finally, bind the stems neatly together with floral tape.*

*Some examples of floral and herbal symbolism:*

*Rose – love*

*Pink – sweetness, fragrance "how sweet you are"*

*Chrysanthemum – friendship*

*Pansy – thoughts*

*Variegated ivy – fidelity*

*Sage – domestic virtue, wisdom*

*Thyme – courage, strength*

*Mint – eternal refreshment*

*Marjoram – blushes, delicate pleasures*

# Raffia Hat

*Warmer springtime weather means that hats no longer have to be purely practical, worn just to keep the wind and snow at bay. Straw and raffia can be decorated with fresh leaves and spring flowers in seasonal yellows and blues to greet the Easter weekend and prospect of summer. This hat has been made from coiled braids of natural raffia, and is encircled with ivy and spring pansies.*

## MATERIALS

- large bundle of natural raffia
- pair of sharp scissors
- bodkin
- two or three long strands of ivy
- bunch of fresh pansies or other colorful flowers

**1** *Begin by tying six strands of raffia together in a knot. Braid the strands together, divided into groups of two.*

**2** *Join on new lengths of raffia by tying the ends together tightly. Continue braiding, tucking in the ends as you go. You will probably need about 8¾–11 yards of braided raffia for the completed hat, so continue until you have about this length.*

**3** *To make the crown, measure the circumference of your head. Take the knotted end of the raffia braid, and coil it to form a round. Stitch each row to the previous one with one strand of raffia threaded on a bodkin. Stitch and coil until you have a round that matches your head circumference.*

**4** *To make the side band, stitch the next row at right angles to the edge of the crown part. Continue to add more rows until a cylinder shape has formed, and the side measures 4 inches.*

**5** *To form the brim, you will have to work the raffia rows outward at an angle of about 45° to the side. Gently ease out each row so it is a little larger than the last. Lay the hat flat on your work surface to stitch on the final rows of the upturned brim.*

**6** *You can make the brim as big as you wish. Finish it off by neatly oversewing the ends of the braid. Trim away any untidy ends.*

**7** ***To decorate and trim the hat****, bind a strand of raffia around a long sprig of ivy, adding in the pansies as you go. Keep adding in ivy and flowers until you have a wreath large enough to go round the hat. Tie the raffia ends together to form a ring.*

**8** *Place the raffia and pansy trim around the brim of the hat. As the flowers will last only a day, there is no need to fix the trim on permanently.*

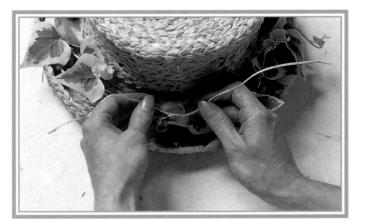

# Handwoven Rustic Willow Basket

*The gloriously random effect of handwoven willow makes a charming nesty feel – perfect for an Easter centerpiece. Fill it with spring flowers, moss, or dyed eggs for the celebration weekend, then afterward substitute other favorite natural decorations to last the seasons through or fill it with fruit. It can also be used as a planter for the garden.*

## MATERIALS

- large bundle of willow or other thin twigs
- pair of sharp scissors or pruning shears

**1** *Soak the willow or twigs in water overnight. Cut five lengths of willow or twig about 24 inches long. Hold the twigs together at the center, two horizontally and three vertically. Take a thin, pliable twig, and weave from the center outward, under and over the crossed twigs. This will hold the other twigs in place.*

**2** *Splay out the first five twigs, and bend them slightly to form the curved ribs of the basket. Carefully weave in a second willow twig, tucking the ends in between the previous rows.*

**3** *Continue adding fresh twigs and weaving them between the ribs. Each row will become wider than the last, and will start to form the basket shape.*

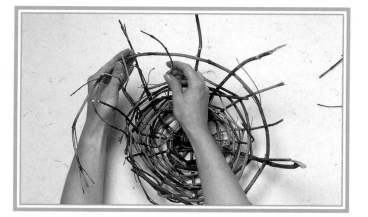

 **4** *To form the handles, bend a 14-inch piece of willow into a U-shape, and carefully slot it in between the woven rows at each side of the basket.*

**5** *Finish off the top edge by bending the end of each rib at right angles to itself, and tucking the ends underneath the last row of weaving.*

# Handmade Paper

*Each handmade sheet of paper is unique, and can be used to make unusual picture frames, stationery, wrappings, boxes, and envelopes. Handmade paper incorporating flowers and leaves is surprisingly easy to make. Lavender or thyme will lend it an aromatic quality, and petals, ferns, and grasses can be added to provide color and texture.*

## MATERIALS

- 2 pieces of plywood, each 10 × 12 inches
- shallow plastic tray
- 3 large sheets of newspaper
- thin, absorbent kitchen cloths
- sheets of waste paper, such as newspaper, photocopy paper and old envelopes
- electric blender
- plastic dishwashing bowl
- flower petals, lavender, ferns, herbs, and grasses

**1** *Make a couching mound to ease the transfer of the layers of paper pulp from the mold to the couching cloths. Lay a plywood rectangle in the shallow tray. Fold the newspaper into varied sizes, and place on top of the plywood. Cover with a kitchen cloth, and moisten with water*

**2** *Half-fill the blender jug with water, and put in two handfuls of waste paper, torn into pieces about 1 inch square. Blend for 10–20 second bursts, add your plant materials and blend again for 5 seconds. Pour four or five jugs of pulp into the dishwashing bowl, and top with water to half capacity.*

## MATERIALS

FOR THE MOLD AND DECKLE

- 6-foot length of
  ¾ × ¾-inch wood
- saw
- waterproof glue
- nails
- 12-inch square of
  nylon curtain mesh
- staple gun

### Making a Mold and Deckle

*An essential piece of paper-making equipment is the mold and deckle. The mold is a rectangular frame of wood with fine mesh stretched across it, while the deckle is an identical frame without the mesh that sits on top of the mesh side of the mold. They can be bought, but to make your own, cut the wood into four 10-inch and four 8-inch lengths.*

*Glue the pieces together to form two rectangles of exactly the same size, butting the edges neatly. When the glue is dry, nail the pieces together. Stretch the nylon mesh over one of the rectangular frames, and use the staple gun to hold it in place. Trim off any excess fabric.*

**3** *Place the wooden deckle on top of the mesh side of the mold, holding both together at each side, and insert into the pulp mixture at an angle of about 45°. Draw both horizontally up through the pulp.*

**4** *When you lift the mold and deckle out of the water, a layer of paper pulp will have been deposited on the mesh. Hold for a few seconds over the bowl to let the water drain away. Remove the deckle, and place the pulp-covered mesh side of the mold on the couching mound.*

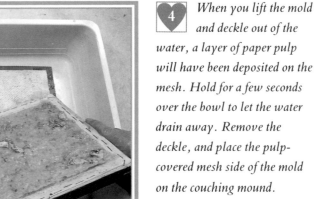

### Picture frame
*Cut a rectangular window in one of the handmade sheets. Fix this to a piece of thick card on three sides only. Leave the lower edge free to insert your picture.*

*Lift the mold, leaving the pulp layer on the mound. Cover with another damp kitchen cloth, and repeat the whole process again. Build up 8–10 layers, then place the other plywood rectangle on top. Squeeze the plywood pieces together to remove the excess water. Peel off the kitchen cloths with the pulp*

*layers attached, and let dry. Remove the paper sheet from the cloth when it is completely dry.*

# Valentine Cards

*It has become customary to exchange cards on Valentine's Day, and it is a more personal gesture to make your own. Let the flowers and leaves in the fields make up your Valentine's cards by pressing them, backing them with thin card, then mounting on fine colored corrugated card. Ivies make a charming natural heart shape; you can either use a single leaf and cut out a heart, or arrange five together to make a single heart outline.*

## MATERIALS

- fresh pansies and ivy leaves
- flower press
- colored corrugated card in rectangles
- craft knife
- PVA glue
- plain paper
- pair of sharp scissors
- double-sided adhesive pads

### Advance preparation

*Press the flowers ahead, so they have time to dry properly. Use a flower press, or simply put the flowers and leaves between the pages of a telephone directory, and place a weight on top. Leave them completely undisturbed for about two weeks.*

**1** ♥ *For the ivy leaf card, score a square of card, and fold in half, then cut out a window in the front. Glue a piece of plain paper behind the window, and then glue on the ivy leaf. Using a craft knife, cut out a tiny heart at the center of the leaf, and then cut away the plain paper from around the leaf.*

**2** ♥ *For the pressed pansy card, glue the pressed pansies in a ring onto plain paper, and cut out carefully with a pair of scissors. Fix the pansy ring to the front of a folded plain card with double-sided adhesive pads to create a three-dimensional effect.*

# Rose Petal Confetti

*What could be more romantic than real rose petals for confetti? Their random sizes, soft, natural colors, and delicate perfume bring them into a different league from the more usual paper variety, and add a perfect touch to a special day. These rose petals have been dried in silica gel crystals so that they retain their shape, color, and fragrance, and they will cause no harm to the environment as tissue confetti sometimes does. Pack the confetti in pretty boxes, and tie with ribbons, raffia or colored string.*

## MATERIALS

- full-blown roses, about 2 per box
- silica gel crystals
- small ovenproof dish
- spoon
- large sheet of petal paper (use commercially available petal paper or make your own – see page 29)
- small sheet of thin card
- pair of sharp scissors
- double-sided sticky tape
- paper punch
- 12-inch piece of ribbon for a small box,
- 16-inch piece of ribbon for a large box

**1** *Remove the rose petals from the stems. Sprinkle a layer of silica gel crystals into the base of a small ovenproof dish, and add a layer of rose petals. Cover with more crystals. Continue layering until the dish is full and the petals are completely covered.*

**2** *Place in an oven set at the lowest temperature, and leave for about 20 minutes. Check at intervals. When the petals are dry, the silica will turn white. Remove from the oven, and let cool for about 10 minutes. Remove the petals from the dish – the excess powder can easily be tapped from the petals.*

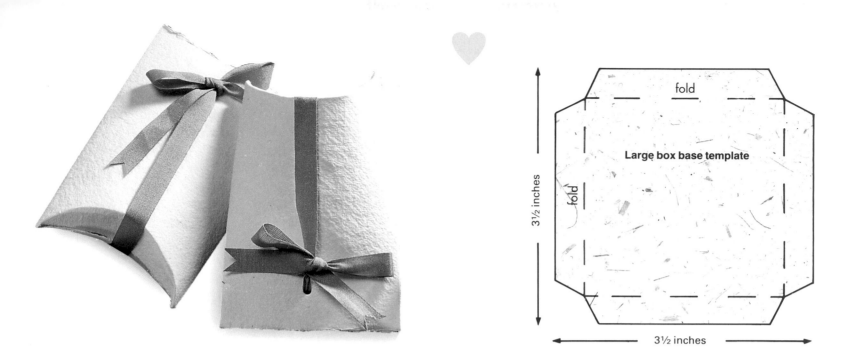

Large box base template

3½ inches

3½ inches

fold

fold

Enlarge templates on a
photocopier by 25%

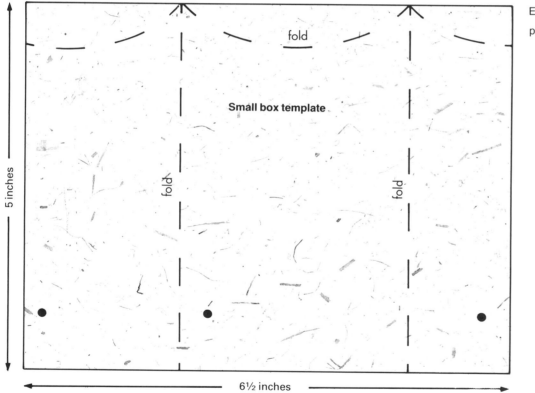

fold

fold

fold

Small box template

5 inches

6½ inches

**3** *To make the large box, cut a rectangle 8 x 12-inch from the large sheet of petal paper, using the template on page 35 to cut the bottom. Fold the short edges of the rectangle to the center, and overlap by ½ inch. Fix the overlap in place with double-sided sticky tape.*

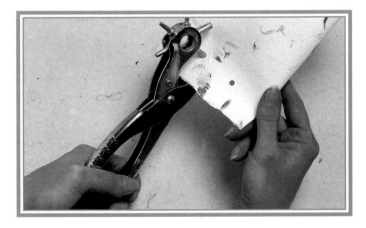

**4** *Using the paper punch, make two holes at the top opening for the ribbon bow.*

 **5** *Trace and enlarge the template for the bottom. Transfer to card and cut out. Score and fold along the dotted lines of the base. Fix the bottom into the box with double-sided sticky tape. Fill the box with confetti, then thread the ribbon through the punched holes and tie with a bow.*

***For the small box***
*Cut out the box shape using the template on page 35. Score along the dotted lines. Fold the sides inward to overlap at the center, and fix with double-sided sticky tape. Use a paper punch to make a hole at the center of the top edge. Fold the curved semi-circular sections to form the bottom, and fix with double-sided sticky tape. Fill the box with confetti, and tie with a ribbon bow.*

# Summer

Summertime is when nature wears her prettiest mantle – the verdant countryside is decked in a succession of subtle shades – and growth is at its fastest now. The race is on to capture the harvest for material both to use now and to preserve for later in the year.

lorious summer! How rich the variety that nature offers now. There seems no end to the variety of flower forms and shades. Delicate heads of Queen Anne's lace dance in the fields, shy wild roses nestle in the hedgerows, gardens boast the extrovert full-blown blooms of roses and peonies; herbs and honeysuckle scent the air; and the trees are fully clothed in a rich mantle of deep green. Nature is at her prime. The colors and forms seem so much more varied now than in the spring. Pinks are a favorite shade, from rich crimsons, to the faintest blush on roses, to poppies, pinks, sweet peas, and peonies; and in the fields, on clover and pink-tinged daisies. The blues follow in larkspur, love-in-a-mist, monkshood and buddleia. There are oranges too, in marigolds, yarrow, and tansy. The growth in early summer is astonishing. As the spring bulbs die down, delicate shoots and buds appear almost unnoticed, then burst into an abundance of color, putting on their greatest effort before the heat of high summer parches the ground, petals fall and all the strength of many plants goes into developing the fruits. Now is the time to gather flowers from the garden to use fresh, to dry or to press. Field flowers are best left to bloom and seed where they are – many are protected, and few survive the journey home after being picked anyway. Young twigs and branches, too, are beautifully pliable at this time of year, offering the perfect material for forming into heart shapes and wreath bases, as well as decorative garden supports and garden screens.

Summer is also the time to beachcomb for the fabulous sculpted shapes of weathered driftwood and for seashells that can be used later to decorate pots, boxes, window boxes, tables, and even clothes and furnishings.

## SUMMER CELEBRATIONS

The lack of traditional celebrations in summer is more than made up for by the number of personal celebrations. This is the favorite season for weddings and christenings, and nature's abundance provides for the decorations: flowers and leaves are woven into garlands, bouquets, posies, and headdresses. But many of the summer country crafts are not linked to celebration, but more to the preservation of the great wealth of natural materials.

## POTPOURRI

It is difficult to resist scooping up fallen rose petals – somehow at the end of their life, they take on an even greater beauty with their colors softening and yet somehow deepening. If you let them dry, laid out on trays in a warm, dry place, they can become a main ingredient for potpourri, bringing a fresh reminder of your summer garden, even in the cold winter months. Lavender, too, with its pungent aromatic scent, and its flowers that are easily dried on trays, can become a valuable ingredient of potpourri.

## PRESERVING FLOWERS AND HERBS

Pressing flowers and leaves was a favored hobby among Victorian young ladies, and it seems such a simple way to preserve plant life that it's almost irresistible for anyone who loves the country. The flatter flowers and leaves produce the best results, because the fleshier or more multi-petaled varieties can begin to rot before all the moisture has been removed. Pick them in late morning after the dew has dried, but before the sun has had time to fade the blooms. Next, lay them between two newspapers on a hard floor or table. Pile on plenty of large books, and leave for a couple of days before checking their progress. The plants are ready when they appear completely flat and dry. If space is at a premium, it may be worth investing in a special flower press, which consists of several layers of blotter paper between two pieces of wood that can be screwed down to provide pressure. The advantage is that several flowers, each placed between a layer of blotter paper, can be pressed at once, and the whole thing is portable. When pressed, flowers can be used to make pictures, or to decorate lampshades, candles, bookmarks, or greetings cards.

There are many varieties of flower that are easy to grow, and would almost dry on the stem if you just left them in the garden. However, if you do that, you risk rot, mildew and damage by animals. Look especially for statice *(Limonium)*, strawflower *(Helichrysum)*, and yarrow *(Achillea)*. Many seedsmen now sell dried flower collections, sometimes even in color themes, making choosing very easy. At harvest time, remember each day to pick and prepare because individual stems can go over in even one day. They are ready to pick when the flowers have just opened, but before they have begun to fade, and the best time to pick them is about mid-morning when all the dew has dried, but before the hot sun has had time to fade the color. Cut each stem using sharp pruning shears, then strip off the leaves as they retain moisture and can rot the stem. Make small bunches and hold them with elastic bands, which naturally tighten as the stems dry and shrink. Hang the

bunches upside down in a dry area with plenty of air circulating. Within a couple of weeks, the flowers will have dried and be ready for use.

Denser, more fleshy flowers, such as roses, peonies, and larkspur are much more difficult to dry. Any home method is really a matter of trial and error, and certainly if you used the air method, they would rot before drying. The best solution is to use a desiccant such as silica gel, which is sold in crystal form at a pharmacy. Sprinkle a layer of silica gel into an airtight box. Lay in the blooms, making sure there's plenty of space around them, and carefully sprinkle more silica gel crystals between the petals. Completely cover the blooms with crystals before sealing the box and placing it in a dry place. The flowers should be ready in about two days. Another successful way of preserving plant material is to use glycerol, which is particularly successful for leaves as they are left supple, though usually tinged a coppery brown. Prepare the material by stripping off the lower leaves, then cutting each stem at a sharp angle. Woody stems should be split and hammered to make sure they take up plenty of liquid. Stand the stems in water for a few hours to insure this. Next, make up a solution of 40 percent glycerol, 60 percent hot water. Stand the leaves in this to a depth of 3–4 inches, and place in a cool, dark place for around six days until they are ready. The idea is that as the mixture is taken up, the water content evaporates, leaving the leaves saturated with glycerol. When completed, the leaves make delightful everlasting greenery to take you through the winter, and even into the spring.

## BEACHCOMBING

There are few things more pleasing than the natural sculpture of old driftwood crafted by the sea, wind, and weather. In just a few months, it is weathered to a soft gray; the sharp edges are rounded; and it is left on the shore neither needed nor wanted, ready for the gleaning. Shells, too, are exquisite weatherproof forms that make marvelous crafting materials both in the home and garden. Their endless forms and textures, from the smooth, shiny surface of tiny cowries to the fabulously ridged, spiked quality of some of the conches, provide great variety in a range of colors, from bleached white through to salmon pink, grays, and browns. It's almost impossible to resist collecting them, a pastime that will keep children happy for hours. However, there are some countries that have banned taking anything off the shore, so be careful before you plunder! Ironically, the hot sunny days that draw us toward the shore in the summer are not the best time for shell-hunting. It is stormy seas that produce the most bounty, bringing in shells and driftwood from farther out at sea. But shores are not the only source of shells. Fish vendors can supply fabulous pickings of shells: mussels, oysters, scallops, and clams, all of which can be turned into exquisite gifts. Arrange them in mosaics, then fix them to tabletops, flowerpots, window boxes, or just make them into a picture to hang on the wall. The best way to fix shells to almost any surface is with a hot glue gun. This gives you a few seconds to adjust the placement if necessary, yet still sticks firm.

Shells can also be used as beads, following a long tradition of many cultures in Africa, Southeast Asia, and the Polynesian Islands, where they are used to decorate fabrics and clothing, even bags and belts. Drilling beads for stitching can be time consuming and fiddly, so many craft suppliers sell them predrilled and ready for use.

# Pressed Flower Wall hanging

*In this raw silk wallhanging, real flowers and leaves have been pressed and woven into the fabric for a breathtakingly natural wall hanging. It is most effective if you choose flowers with naturally vibrant colors, such as blue scabious, yellow chrysanthemums, and the delicate lilac of the common mallow because their tones fade as they dry. The bay leaves used for the edges offer a natural aroma to scent the room.*

## MATERIALS

- 20 × 32-inch rectangle of loosely woven raw silk fabric
- bodkin
- 1½ × 4-inch piece of stiff acetate film
- selection of pressed flowers and 8 dried bay leaves
- long metal skewer
- PVA glue
- paper punch
- 22-inch length of bamboo

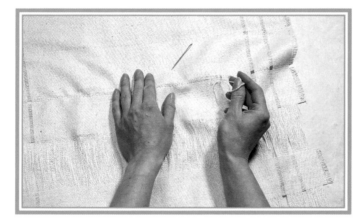

**1** *Lay the silk flat, and use a bodkin to draw out the horizontal threads from the fabric for 6 inches at the lower edge. Draw out four 3-inch wide bands of thread at 2-inch intervals. Next draw out six vertical threads 1¼ inches in from each side and again 1¼ inches in from that.*

**2** *Fold the acetate rectangle in half, and place a pressed flower inside.*

**3** *Weave the skewer under alternate threads along the horizontal bands. Lift the skewer to separate the threads, then insert the acetate between the fibers. Hold the pressed flower inside the acetate, then carefully pull the film away, leaving the flower between the fibers. When the flowers are in place, turn the*

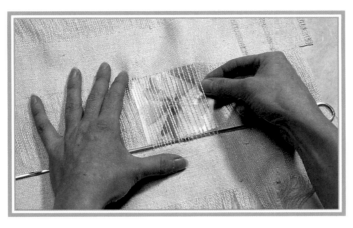

*wallhanging over, and hold each flower in place with glue.*

**4** *Let the glue dry before moving the wallhanging again. Turn the wallhanging over to the right side. Take the dried bay leaves and, using the paper punch, make two small holes at the center of each.*

**5** *Tie a bay leaf to the vertical threads at each end of the horizontal bands. Use the threads that have been drawn out, and finish each with a tiny bow.*

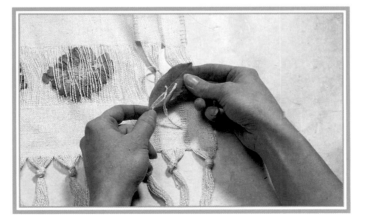

**6** *Using a couple of the drawn threads, neaten the raw edges at each side with a row of blanket stitch.*

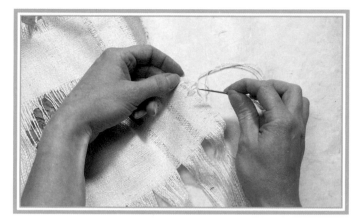

**7** *Separate the fringe at the lower edge into groups about ¾ inch wide. Tie each group in a knot.*

**8** *Turn a ½-inch hem to the wrong side along the top edge, then turn another 2 inches over. Slip stitch in place to form the casing for the bamboo. Insert the bamboo, then thread several of the drawn threads through the hanging and under the bamboo cane at each end to make a hanging loop.*

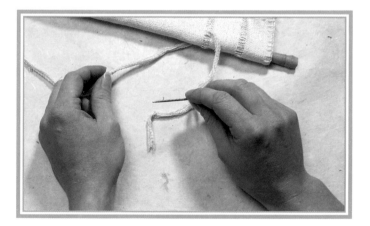

# Fresh Herb Wreath

*In some north European countries, a herb wreath hung in the kitchen or on the door is a sign of welcome. Just like any flower arrangement, it will stay fresh for several days, but, unlike most, it can also be preserved for future use. Simply remove the bunches of herbs, and hang them upside down to dry. When dried, they can be used for flavoring dishes for many months to come. Summer is the best time to pick herbs. Take them at midday and preferably before they flower.*

## MATERIALS

- thick plastic-coated garden wire
- selection of fresh herbs, such as sage, mint, tarragon, thyme, marjoram, rosemary, and dill
- medium-gauge floral wire on a spool
- wire cutter

**1** *Cut a 1-yard length of thick garden wire. Arrange the herbs in separate bunches on your work surface. Taking a sprig from each bunch, bind together in a small bundle with floral wire from the spool. Bind the bundle to the base wire about 4 inches from the end.*

**2** *Repeat the process with a second bundle of herbs, binding them onto the base wire but slightly overlapping the first.*

3 *Continue to attach more bundles in this way until the base wire is covered. Leave about 4 inches free at the end. Twist the ends of the base wire together to complete the ring. Bind on another bundle of herbs to cover the join if necessary.*

# Natural Toiletries

*Before cosmetics and beauty products were available commercially, people made their own from natural flowers, plants, herbs, and spices. Package some bathtime toiletries such as these bath herbs in tiny hessian sacks trimmed with ribbon or some nature-inspired shell soap and a facecloth tied around with string. They may be the simplest of gifts, but beautifully presented, they'll bring infinite pleasure.*

## MATERIALS

#### FOR THE SHELL SOAP
- 1 bar of unscented soap
- grater
- heatproof bowl
- large clam shell
- cotton facecloth
- natural string

#### FOR THE BATH SALTS
- 1½ cups natural sea salt
- 3 tablespoons dried lavender
- lavender essential oil
- wooden box
- white emulsion
- medium-grade sandpaper
- clam shell
- 12 × 4¾ inch piece of hessian
- 12-inch piece of ribbon

 **For the shell soap,** grate the bar of soap into a heatproof bowl. Add a few teaspoons of boiling water, and mix into the soap. The hot water will make the soap soft and easy to mold. Pile the soft soap into the clam shell, and press down with your fingers.

**2** Let the soap cool, then remove from the mold. Tie the soap into a little package with a cotton facecloth and natural string.

## Bath salts

*Mix together the sea salt and the dried lavender. Add a few drops of the lavender essential oil. Keep the salts in a pretty box or hessian bag.*

## MATERIALS

FOR THE BATH LOTION
- 1 tablespoon dried lavender flowers
- 1 tablespoon dried basil
- pinch of cinnamon powder
- 1¼ cups witch hazel
- glass bottle

## Bath lotion

*Mix together the dried lavender and basil in a glass bottle. Add a pinch of cinnamon, and fill the bottle to the top with witch hazel. Seal the bottle tightly, and shake well. Let steep for at least two weeks, shaking occasionally. The witch hazel will turn a golden color. Strain the mixture, and discard the herbs. Rinse the bottle, and refill with the bath lotion. You can top up the bottle with more witch hazel if required.*

**1** ***For the hessian bag*** *take a 12 × 4¾-inch piece of hessian. Draw out about four threads along each short side, about 2 inches down from the raw edges.*

**2** *Fold the hessian piece in half, and stitch each side. Turn the bag through to the right side, and fill with salts. Thread a ribbon through the drawn-out section, and tie securely with a bow.*

### For the box

*We used an old cigar box. Paint your box with white emulsion, and when it has dried, rub the surface with medium-grade sandpaper to achieve a distressed look. Glue on a pretty clam shell to decorate the lid.*

# Kitchen Herbs

*Gather up the last of the summer herbs to dry and package as gifts. Fresh or dried herbs are essential ingredients in cooking, and add flavor to traditional and exotic dishes alike. Two classic combinations are the "bouquet garni," a string-tied bundle containing bay, parsley, and thyme, and "Herbes de Provence," a mixture of oregano, thyme, savory, marjoram, basil, and rosemary.*

## MATERIALS

### DRIED BOUQUET GARNI

- 20 dried bay leaves
- sharp pair of scissors
- 3 heaped tablespoons each of dried thyme and parsley
- 1 tablespoon of dried celery leaves
- 8-inch square piece of cheesecloth for each package
- ball of string
- paper punch
- airtight jar

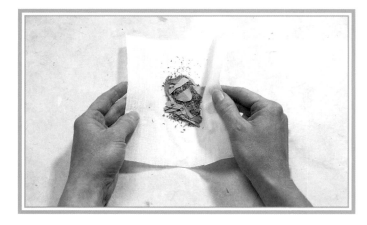

**1** ***For dried bouquet garni,*** *snip 10 of the dry bay leaves into pieces, using a sharp pair of scissors. Mix them together with the other dry ingredients in a small bowl. Place a spoonful of the dry mixture in the center of a cheesecloth square. Wrap the cheesecloth around the herbs like a little package.*

**2** *Tie up the package with string. Using the paper punch, punch two holes in the middle of a dried bay leaf, and tie it with a double knot to each package. Make about 10 packages in this way, and store in an airtight jar ready for use.*

## MATERIALS

### HERBES DE PROVENCE

- 4 × 16-inch rectangle of cheesecloth for each sachet
- pair of sharp scissors
- matching sewing thread
- sewing needle
- 2 tablespoons each of dried oregano, thyme, savory, marjoram, basil, and rosemary
- 10-inch piece of ribbon for each sachet
- small piece of card for a label

**1** ***For herbes de Provence,*** *take a cheesecloth rectangle, and fold it in half. Stitch the two long sides together with matching sewing thread. Turn the bag through to the right side.*

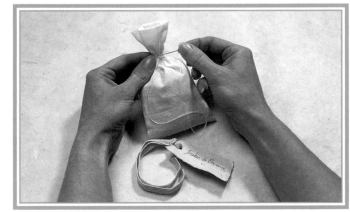

**2** *Fold a 2-inch hem to the wrong side along the raw edge at the opening of the bag. Mix all the dry ingredients in a bowl, then place a few spoonfuls in the bag. The mixture is enough for about five bags. Tie the bag securely with a ribbon, and label clearly.*

## MATERIALS

### FRESH BOUQUET GARNI

- 2 to 3 bay leaves
- 1 sprig each of fresh thyme and parsley
- 3-inch piece of celery
- ball of string

**1** ***For fresh bouquet garni,*** *take the herbs and celery, and tie securely with a piece of string.*

Herbes de Provence

Herbes de Provence

Bouquet Garni

# Pressed Herb Montage

*A delightful picture to make for the kitchen – six pressed herbs, individually mounted, are arranged to form a chart. The blue-green paper backing perfectly complements the natural blue and silver tones of many herbs, while offsetting their delicate filigree forms.*

## MATERIALS

- selection of fresh herbs, such as sage, thyme, marjoram, parsley, tarragon, or rosemary
- flower press or telephone directory
- paintbrush
- PVA glue
- 6 small rectangles of handmade rag paper, approximately 5 × 7 inches
- blue-green paper backing
- picture frame

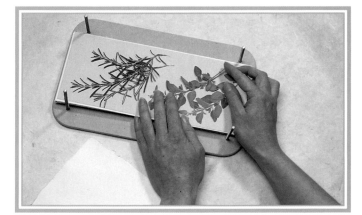

**1** *Select the best sprigs from each herb, and press them in a flower press or a telephone directory for at least two weeks. When dry, remove from the press or telephone directory very carefully; otherwise you could damage the delicate leaves.*

**2** *Using a small paintbrush, paint glue onto the herb sprig, and carefully press onto the rag paper backing. Arrange the herbs on the paper backing and insert into the picture frame.*

# Shell Candles

*Shells make brilliant natural candleholders, providing a wonderful warm glow close to the table where you need it. The addition of citronella essential oil will give insect-repellant properties, ideal on warm summer evenings. Put one at each place setting, or scatter them liberally around the table. The small candles, scented with essential oil, quickly liquefy, providing a pool of wax in their shell as they burn.*

## MATERIALS

- selection of large seashells from abalones, oysters, and clams
- quick-drying heat-resistant filler
- wooden skewer
- candlewick
- removable adhesive tack
- large candles
- heat-resistant bowl

**1** First fill any holes in the shell with quick-drying filling paste or cement. Use the wooden skewer to push the filler into any small holes, and let dry completely.

**2** Cut a 4-inch length of candlewick. Fix one end into the base of the shell with removable tack, and wind the other end around the wooden skewer. The skewer will keep the wick upright while the wax is poured in.

**3** Cut the candles into 1¼-inch long pieces, and place in a heat-resistant bowl. Put the bowl in a moderately hot oven until the wax has melted. Remove the old wicks and discard. Spoon the melted wax into the shell, and let it cool. You can add a few drops of essential oil while the wax is still melted.

**Safety note**
Never leave candles to burn unattended, and always place them on a heat-resistant surface.

# Shell Mobile

*Shells, string, and driftwood are a pleasing combination that have been used here to produce this beautiful natural mobile. The trick is to find a pair of complementary pieces of driftwood because cutting them to size would completely spoil the effect. The mobile can be hung by a window, or outside where it will become a beautiful, natural windchime.*

## MATERIALS

- power drill with a fine drill bit
- assorted seashells
- thick piece of wood
- 2 pieces of driftwood, approximately the same size
- ball of fine string

**1** *Drill a hole at the top and bottom edge of each shell. To prevent the drill from slipping, use a thick piece of wood on top of the work surface. Drill four holes through each piece of driftwood.*

**2** *Thread the shells onto the string, making a small knot at each side to keep them in place. Thread the ends of each string through the driftwood and tie. Check the mobile is balanced, and tie on small shells to compensate for any unevenness. Make the central two strings into a hanging loop.*

# Ice Bowl

*Make a decorative cooler-cum-table centerpiece by freezing fresh scabious flower heads in a bowl of ice. It's a delightful idea, which will always look good because the blooms will be perfectly preserved in the ice, and will naturally complement the season's colors. If you wish to use the bowl outdoors, stand it in a shady spot. This spectacular ice bowl can also be used for serving ice cream and fruits for a summer dinner party.*

## MATERIALS

- about 20 scabious flower heads or any other flower of your choice
- pair of sharp scissors
- 2 glass bowls of similar shape, one 3 pints and one 4 pints in capacity
- glass jar filled with sand
- jug

**1** *Snip the stem off each flower close to the head. Place the flowers face outward to line the inside of the larger glass bowl. Place the smaller bowl inside, and weigh it down with the sand-filled jar.*

**2** *Pour cold water into the space between the two bowls. Place in a freezer until the water has completely frozen. To remove the ice bowl, simply run warm water over the outside of the larger bowl, and rinse the inside of the smaller bowl. The surface of the ice should melt just enough for you to turn it out.*

# Lavender Bottles

*In Victorian times nearly every young lady knew how to weave ribbon round fresh lavender to make lavender bottles. When finished, they dry naturally, and make a perfect linen freshener, either scattered in lingerie drawers or hung with clothes in a closet. They're not difficult to make, but can be time-consuming, which is why you'll rarely find lavender bottles in the stores today.*

## MATERIALS

- about 15 fresh lavender stems (always use an odd number)
- sewing thread
- a pair of sharp scissors
- 1 yard of ¼-inch wide satin ribbon
- sewing needles

**1** *Tie the lavender stems tightly together with sewing thread just below the flower heads.*

**2** *Carefully bend the flower stems back over the flower heads to form a little cage.*

3 *Stitch one end of the ribbon to the lower end of the cage. Weave the ribbon under and over the flower stems until the flowers are completely encased. Pull the ribbon quite tightly at the top, and stitch in place. Tie on a ribbon bow and hanging loop.*

# Hinged Shell Trinket Boxes

*Natural shells can be hinged together to make enchanting trinket boxes –*
*perfect also for keeping rings and other small items of jewelry overnight.*
*Group them on your dressing table or mantelpiece to provide a pretty yet*
*practical decoration.*

## MATERIALS

- large scallop shell or
  lucina shell
- sheet of medium-grade
  sandpaper
- PVA glue
- small brass hinge

**1** *Wash and dry the shell carefully. Place the two halves together to give you an indication of where the hinge should be positioned. Rub the surface of the shell at the hinge position with sandpaper. This will smooth the area, and provide a good surface for the glue to adhere to.*

**2** *Glue one side of the hinge into position and let the glue set firmly. Glue the other side in place. Set the box to one side, and let the glue set completely before flexing the hinge.*

# $f$all

NOW IS THE TIME OF TRUE ABUNDANCE WHEN THE FRUIT IS HEAVY ON THE TREES AND THE HARVEST ALMOST HOME. EVEN AS NATURE PREPARES FOR REPOSE, SHE PUTS ON A FIERY SHOW WITH THE COPPERY TONES OF FALL. THERE'S STILL PLENTY OF FRESH MATERIAL AROUND TO BE USED OR PRESERVED, AND NATURE HAS ALREADY DONE A LOT OF HER OWN PRESERVATION, PROVIDING ENDLESS PINECONES, SEEDCASES, AND NUTS. TRADITIONALLY, FALL IS THE FINEST TIME TO COLLECT NATURAL CRAFT MATERIAL.

fall must be the most voluptuous season: it's the time when everything finally comes into fruition; the season that's overflowing with riches. Gone is the exhausting heat of late summer, when the ground looked parched and the last of the flowers seemed to have passed away. Welcome are the cooler mornings bringing the new, flamboyant fall blooms in yellows and golds, oranges and rusts along with an astounding offering of ripening fruits in the orchard. Apples and pears in golds, russets, greens, and reds vie with purple plums, lightly dusted with a soft bloom, and bright shiny clusters of blackberries scrambling through the hedgerows. Berries, often in vibrant oranges, hang in pendulous branches, decorating trees and shrubs. Out in the fields, the harvest is truly home. The wheat, universally symbolic of harvest and fall, is gathered in. Pumpkins and squashes, in their astonishingly voluptuous, overblown forms, pile up around farm buildings and in the market place. The air is scented with the honeyed perfume of ripened fruit so abundant, it almost seems to burden its trees. The damp misty mornings seem to emphasize the effect, giving way to very mild days even in northern climes. Nature seems almost to be offering up its final burst of energy in an astounding display before going to sleep for winter. Even some of the flowers that have long dropped their petals, manage to leave behind a rich legacy of graceful seedcases – the familiar globes of poppy heads or the spiky remains of teasles, thistles, and love-in-a-mist.

This is the season that offers the richest choice of natural material simply waiting to be gathered in. Traditionally, it was the season in which everyone worked hardest. The race to bring everything in was matched by the race to preserve it all for winter. Now is the time to search out seedcases, pick up pinecones on country walks, gather in the last of the petals for pressing and drying, harvest the fall fruits for preserving and pickling, and turn them into decorations for the home, gifts for Christmas, or seasonal displays.

## Fall Celebrations

For all communities until recently, the outcome of the harvest was literally a matter of life and death. A bad harvest could mean a very difficult winter and, in some cases, even famine. So it's little wonder that the harvest has been celebrated by communities throughout the world since cultivation began. In Europe during the harvest festival, usually sometime in early October, churches and villages are decorated with sheaves of corn, bound together in a variety of ways, and country people bring produce to the church as an offering of thanks for the harvest. Thanksgiving happens later in the year, on the fourth Thursday in November. It was first celebrated in 1621 by the Pilgrim Fathers, who instigated it to give thanks for the safe gathering-in and preserving of their first harvest across the Atlantic. The traditional Thanksgiving meal still mirrors the food that the early Pilgrim Fathers enjoyed: turkey with cranberry sauce, sweet potatoes, and corn bread, followed by pumpkin pie.

Halloween is a much older fall celebration, harking back to pagan times. In the ancient Celtic calendar, October 31 was the last day of the year, the time when people believed the risen souls of the dead roamed the earth causing mischief. Children throughout the western world still acknowledge those heathen roots by dressing up as witches and ghouls on Halloween, then demanding "treats" from householders under threat of a "trick." All this still occurs despite centuries of the Christian celebration of All Saints (also known as All Hallows) Day on November 1, established in an attempt to oust the pagan festival. But whatever the festival, this is the time when pumpkins and squashes reign in all their variations, from the near garish oranges to cool greens, and even white.

## Making the Food Last

Traditionally, preserving the harvest was the top priority of fall; otherwise the prospect of winter could be very grim indeed. Nowadays, although modern refrigeration and freezing techniques have superseded this need, there is still a place for bottling, preserving, pickling, and drying. Any gardener, who has nurtured tomato plants through the summer, knows the compulsion to make use of every single fruit before the frost reaches it, even if that does mean using it green. And what owner of a tree laden with fruit can resist the urge to make use of it in preserves or dried for decoration?

Homemade preserves have become such a treat nowadays that they are always welcome gifts. Make them extra special with the packaging, using natural materials to give them an appealing country feel. Cloth tops are not the only option – try wrapping the jars in brown paper held in place with twine, or even fine corrugated card, which takes the shape of the jar well. This can be decorated by tucking something to suggest the contents under the twine – a leaf, dried berries, or petals perhaps. If none of those are suitable, try photocopying an old print or etching of the relevant fruit or vegetable, then cutting out the image to stick onto the paper covering the jar. It should not be too difficult to find relevant images in the local library, which can be copied and enlarged or reduced to the right size on the library photocopier.

Preserves can be made into an even more substantial gift with the addition of a relevant utensil – perhaps a preserve spoon, again tucked into the twine. Oils and vinegars look pretty labeled using hand script on a simple baggage label, decorated with a dried or pressed sprig of the relevant herb. Sachets of dried herbs can also be packaged into a jar and labeled in the same way, or even simply labeled symbolically by tying on a sample of the contents.

## CORN DOLLIES

The tradition of making corn dollies dates back to pagan times, when it was believed that unless the corn spirit was captured before she left the field, there would be a poor crop the next year. People thought she moved through the field in front of the reapers, and came to rest in the last sheaf. When this was cut, it was made into an effigy or dolly, and hung in the farmhouse until the following spring, when it was then taken into the field, and its seed was included in the sowing.

Not all straw is suitable for making corn dollies: the modern varieties of wheat usually have short, stiff stems to withstand the weather. The longer and more pliable the straw, the better for dollies. These older varieties are still grown in many parts of Britain for thatching houses, and suitable material can be sourced through local crafts people. Another way to find good varieties of straw would be through craft suppliers. In the United States, brown corn grown in the central west is a good variety.

If you plan to obtain straw straight from a farmer, you'll need to tell him that it should be cut about three weeks before the harvest when the ears are still pointing upward, the stems are gold, but the nodes or leaf-points still show signs of green. The straw will then have to be prepared for weaving. Make sure it is completely dried out before beginning, then cut the straw about ½ inch above the lowest node. Then, holding the top, pull off the outer leaves. Once all the straw has been stripped in this way, it needs to be graded into sizes – three sizes should be enough, although some people like to grade it further into six.

Before work, the straw will need to be tempered to make it more pliable. Do this by putting it into a bathtub of hot water for about 5 minutes (or 20 minutes in cold water). When it's ready, take the straw out of the bathtub and roll it in a towel until you need it. However, don't leave it damp overnight because it will become discolored and mildewed – dry it off in a warm room on an oven rack to let plenty of air circulate around each straw.

# Corn Dollies

*These ancient fertility symbols date back to pagan times. Farmers believed that if the corn spirit was not captured before the last sheaf of corn was cut, the crops would fail the following year. Thus corn dollies were made from the last sheaf, then hung up in the farmhouse until the next spring when they were planted in the soil with the new seeds. If you can braid, they're not difficult to make, and when finished, provide a pleasing decoration for any room in the home.*

## MATERIALS

- bundle of corn straws, available from craft suppliers
- strong thread
- pair of sharp scissors
- 1 strand of raffia for the Welsh fan
- 20-inch length of ribbon for the Mordiford dolly

### Advance preparation

*Before the straws can be used, they must be tempered. This means that they must be soaked in a bathtub of water for about 20 minutes to insure that the straws are flexible enough not to break while the dolly is being made.*

**1** ***For the Welsh fan,*** *you will need 15 tempered straws for the completed dolly. Take three straws and tie them together tightly just below the ears with strong thread. Spread the stems out on the work surface, two to the right and one to the left.*

**2** *Take a fourth straw and lay it on top of the left-hand straw, but lying parallel to the two right-hand ones. Place a fifth straw under the far right straw and over the others. Bring this straw over to lie parallel with the left-hand straw.*

**3** *Pick up the central right-hand straw, and bend it carefully upward. Bend the first straw around to lie parallel with the left-hand straws.*

**4** *Bring the central straw back to lie flat on the work surface; this will now be on the outside. This action locks in each new straw.*

 **5** *Repeat the process of inserting new straws and locking in on both sides until all the straws have been used. Tie the straws into two bundles at the top with a piece of raffia.*

**1** ***For the Mordiford dolly*** *(named after its place of origin), take five tempered straws, and tie them together with strong thread just below the ears. Hold the ears downward between your forefinger and middle finger. Arrange the stems so that two point north, one south, one east, and one west.*

**2** *Bend the right-hand north straw through 90° to lie on top of the west straw. Rotate the whole thing, so that the two straws that were facing west are now pointing north. Repeat the process, rotating after every fold until you have woven about 6 inches. Tie the stems together and then make another.*

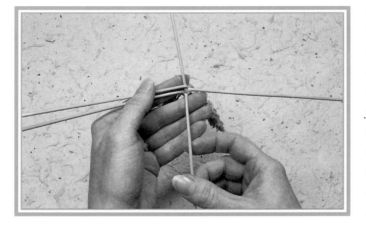

**3** *Keeping the stems at the center, bend the woven parts around to form a heart shape. Tie securely in place with strong thread, then attach a pretty ribbon bow.*

# Pressed Leaf Papier-Mâché Bowl

*Preserved leaves make charming decorations for a simple papier-mâché bowl.*
*The combination of large copper beech tree leaves with delicate herb Robert*
*makes for greater variety. Either press your own in a flower press and leave*
*for a week or two until perfectly dry and flat, or buy ready glyceroled leaves,*
*which offer greater flexibility.*

## MATERIALS

- large shallow bowl to use
  as a mold
- plastic wrap
- plenty of newspaper
- wallpaper paste mixed to
  a soupy consistency
- gesso
- cream emulsion paint
- dark red emulsion paint
- bunch of copper beech
  and herb Robert leaves
- PVA glue
- flowerpress or telephone
  directory
- water-based satin finish
  varnish

 *Line the inside of the bowl with a layer of plastic wrap. Tear the newspaper into strips about 1 inch wide. Brush wallpaper paste onto one side of the newspaper, then smooth it onto the inside of the bowl.*

**2** *Build up eight to ten layers in this way. Make sure that the torn edges overlap the edge of the bowl to form a lip around the edge. Put the bowl in a warm, dry place for several days until the paper has dried completely. Gently prize the papier-mâché away from the mold.*

**3** Lay the bowl upside down on your work surface, and gently roll up the torn edges to form a lip or rim. Paste another layer of paper strips over the rim edge, and let dry.

**4** Coat the entire bowl with a layer of gesso. This acts as a sealant, and masks the newsprint. Coat the inside of the bowl with cream emulsion, and paint the outside and rim dark red. When the emulsion has dried, hand-paint a row of cream dots around the rim.

**5** Follow the instructions on page 32 for pressing flowers and press the leaves. When they are ready, apply a thin layer of glue to each one, and press it gently onto the inside surface of the bowl. When they are firmly fixed, apply three to four coats of quick-drying, water-based satin finish varnish.

**Using varnish**
Quick-drying, water-based varnish appears white when wet but dries clear. Remember to let each coat dry thoroughly before recoating.

# Scented Herb Pillows

*Sleep-inducing herbs such as hops and camomile can be used to fill these delightful hand-embroidered herb pillows. Made from a loose-weave fabric, they allow the aroma to seep through, and can be placed near the bed pillows at night to help relieve stress, offering relaxation at the end of a busy day. Camomile, rosemary, lavender, hops, mint, and basil are all said to have a relaxing effect.*

## MATERIALS

### BUTTONED PILLOW

- 4¾-inch square of checked muslin for the button panel
- 2 9-inch squares of plain muslin fabric
- pair of sharp scissors
- 5 small buttons
- contrasting embroidery thread
- sewing needles and pins
- 2 cups scented herbs

### BOW PILLOW

- 8-inch square of checked muslin
- pair of sharp scissors
- matching sewing thread
- sewing needles and pins
- 2 cups scented herbs

**1** ***For the buttoned pillow***, *place the small checked square of muslin on the center of one of the larger muslin squares. Sew on the five small buttons. Work a row of herringbone stitch around the edge, using contrasting embroidery thread.*

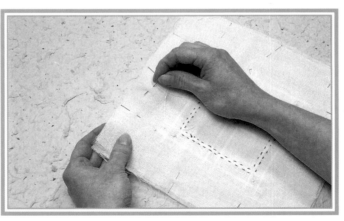

**2** *Pin and stitch the two large muslin squares with right sides together. Leave a small gap in the stitching.*

*Turn the pillow through to the right side. Stitch again with matching thread about ¾ inch in from the edge to create a small flange. Fill the pillow with the herbs.*

 *Work a row of running stitches around the flanged edge with embroidery thread.*

***For the bow pillow***, *make up in exactly the same way as before, but omit the embroidered panel. Instead, add two fabric bows.*

# Fern Print Cushion

*Beautiful designs can be printed on linens and cushions using natural leaves and flowers. Make a plain cushion cover from natural, unbleached calico, and transform it into a work of art with the use of spray paint, masking tape, and a fresh fern. By spraying on the paint, you can achieve a soft dappled effect. The fern acts as a resist, in other words it masks the fabric from the paint and leaves its image in negative on the fabric when removed – almost like a stencil but in reverse.*

## MATERIALS

- 28 inches of 44-inch wide unbleached cotton calico fabric
- pair of sharp scissors
- sewing needles and pins
- matching sewing thread
- masking tape
- large fern
- blue and green spray paints

 *Mask off a 2-inch wide border, using masking tape, from the stitching line inward. Place the fern on the cushion, and pin in position if necessary.*

 *Spray over the cushion lightly with blue spray paint, and then with green spray paint to achieve a mottled effect. Make sure the room is well ventilatd when using spray cans.*

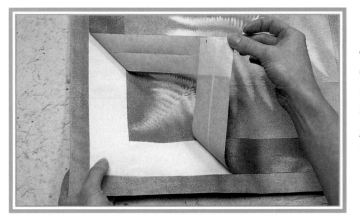

**3** *When the paint has dried, remove the fern and masking tape to reveal the delicate fern pattern. The same type of effect can be achieved by sponging on acrylic or stencil paints, but this would take longer.*

**To make the cushion**

*Cut one 19-inch square from the calico for the front and two 19 x 13½-inch rectangles for the backs. Machine-stitch a narrow double hem along one long edge of both back pieces. Press the hem. Lay the backs on the front, right sides facing, overlapping the hemmed edges in the center, this will become the opening. Machine-stitch all round ⅝ inch from the raw edge. Snip across each corner, and turn the cushion to the right side. Press. Machine-stitch 1¼ inches in from the edge to form a narrow flange.*

85

# Drying Flowers

*Preserve summer's bounty by drying flowers and foliage to use over the winter months. They look fabulous simply hung up in bunches, or they can be used to make imaginative table adornments, wreaths, or wallhangings, for decorating packages or making up winter bouquets. Air-drying is the most natural way to preserve herbs, flowers, and leaves for decorative or culinary uses. Most varieties can be successfully dried in one of two ways, as follows.*

## MATERIALS

- bunch of flowers or herbs
- ball of string
- shallow tray, cardboard box lid or tea tray
- piece of cheesecloth to place over the tray or lid
- sticky tape

### Air circulation

*The reason for using only small bunches at a time is that air has to be able to circulate around the leaves and flowers in order to draw moisture out. Flowers at the center of large bunches tend to stay damp, and can become moldy.*

*1 To air-dry bunches of flowers or herbs, strip the leaves from the lower stems, then gather a few blooms together in a small bunch. Tie the stems tightly together with string, leaving enough string to tie into a hanging loop. Hang the bunches upside down in a warm place until dry.*

*2 To air-dry individual flower heads, petals, or small sprigs, cover a shallow tray with cheesecloth. Fix the cheesecloth in place with sticky tape. Place the flower heads, petals, or herbs on the cheesecloth, and leave in a warm, dry place. Air will circulate all around the plants, and they will dry evenly.*

# Natural Jewelry

*There are a number of natural items that make ideal beads. So why not string together some accessories using fruit seeds and beans. The range of color choices available from the kitchen is amazing. Seek out the charmingly spotted black-eyed peas, lentils, melon or squash skins, dried red kidney beans, fruit seeds, small and large, and string them together on a leather thong or waxed string to make nature's very own jewelry.*

## MATERIALS

- small squash
- sharp knife
- paper towel
- plate
- assorted dried beans such as red kidney beans, black-eyed peas, pinto beans, lima beans, navy beans, lentils
- dried melon seeds, apricot pits
- power drill fitted with a fine bit
- small pliers
- thick piece of wood
- 1 yard fine leather thong or thick waxed necklace cord for each necklace
- pair of sharp scissors
- wires for earrings

**1** *To make beads from squash skin, cut wedges from the squash. Cut away the flesh, and cut the skin into pieces ¾–1¼ inches long. Place on a sheet of paper towel, and leave in a warm, dry place for up to a week. The pieces will curl up as they dry, forming tubes which can be threaded.*

**2** *Dried beans need a small hole drilled through them before use. Use a power drill fitted with a fine bit, and hold the bean firmly with a small pair of pliers on a thick piece of wood. This will get easier with practice. Smaller seeds like melon or pumpkin can usually be pierced with a needle.*

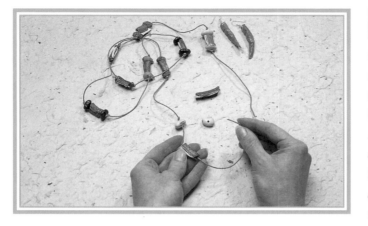

**3** *Thread the squash skin beads onto a fine leather thong interspaced with the beans. Tie knots at intervals along the thong to keep the beads in little groups. Make a pair of earrings by drilling a hole at the top of two long pieces of squash skin and attaching them to silver wires.*

# Potpourri

*Rose petals and lavender flowers are among the few flowers that retain their scent after drying. However, most other ingredients require the use of a fixative substance such as orris root powder, which clings to the leaves or petals and absorbs the scented oils that are mixed with the dry ingredients.*

MATERIALS

ROSE AND LAVENDER
POTPOURRI
- 2 cups of dried rose petals
- 1 cup of dried lavender flowers
- 1 tablespoon of any other fragrant herb
- 1 tablespoon of orris root powder
- 6 drops of rose essential oil or a combination of rose and lavender

AUTUMNAL POTPOURRI
- 3 cups of mixed dry fall leaves and sycamore keys
- few small pinecones
- dried rind of 1 lemon, 1 orange and 1 lime
- 6 drops of bergamot essential oil

 *Gather all the dry ingredients together, and place in a bowl. They can be dried using the method described on page 86. Sprinkle 1 tablespoon of orris root powder over the mixture, and stir well.*

*Add the essential oil, drop-by-drop, stirring well after each drop. Put the potpourri in a sealed container, and leave in a warm, dry place to age for four to six weeks, shaking occasionally. After mixing all potpourris must be aged in a sealed container for four to six weeks for the fragrances to develop.*

# Bean-covered Fruits

*Make some decorative apples and pears, the classic fall orchard fruits.
With fabric bases, they take on a wonderfully colorful, textural look when
covered with red kidney beans, black-eyed peas and seeds. You can also add
aromatic potpourri or lavender to the filling to make them extra special.
Just one would look fun on the mantelpiece, or make several and line them
up as if they were stored in an outhouse for winter.*

See the template on page 93.

## MATERIALS

- 24 x 6-in rectangle of
cotton fabric for a fruit
- pair of sharp scissors
- sewing needles and pins
- matching sewing thread
- natural jute string
- polyester toy stuffing or
potpourri or lavender
- PVA glue
- paintbrush
- assorted dried beans, such
as red kidney beans, black-
eyed peas, and green
pumpkin seeds

**1** *Using the template on
page 93, cut out four
fabric pieces as indicated, so
that the center of the fabric
panel is on the cross grain. Pin
and stitch the pieces together in
pairs, along one curved edge.
Next, open out the stitched
pairs, and place them together
with the right sides facing each
other.*

**2** *Pin around half the
raw edge from the top
to the seam at the bottom. Take
a piece of jute string about 16
inches long, fold in half and
knot each end. Tuck one
knotted end inside the seam at
the bottom. Continue pinning
around the raw edge. Stitch the
pinned seam together, leaving
a small gap at the top edge.*

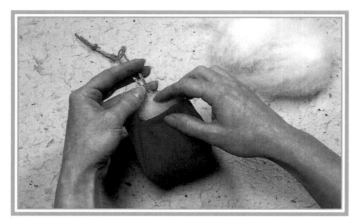

**3** *Turn the fabric shape to the right side. The jute string will now be up through the center of the apple, and will protrude out of the opening at the top. Fill firmly with polyester toy stuffing. Add potpourri or lavender to the stuffing if you wish.*

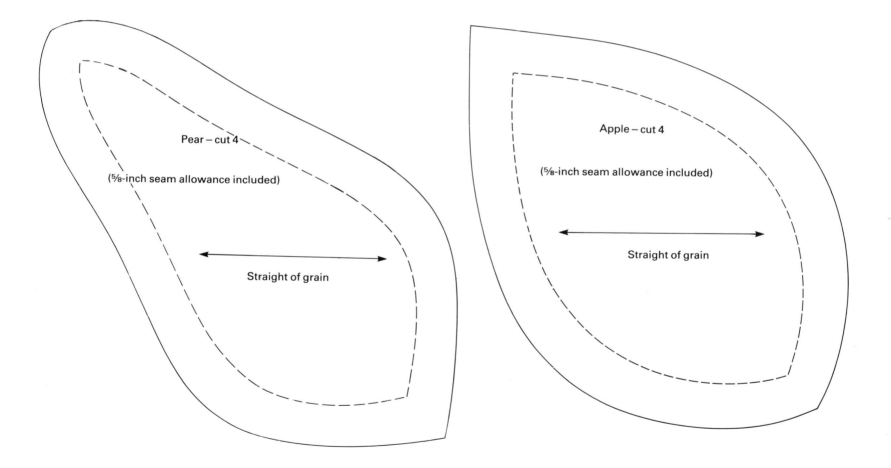

Pear – cut 4

(⅝-inch seam allowance included)

Straight of grain

Apple – cut 4

(⅝-inch seam allowance included)

Straight of grain

  *Using matching sewing thread, slip stitch neatly over the opening of the seam, taking care not to catch the jute string in the stitching.*

 *Pull the string tightly to form a dimple at each end of the apple. Knot the string at the top, close to the seam, so that the apple is held in shape. Trim the end of the string, and knot again.*

*Coat the surface of the fabric apple with a layer of glue. Press dried beans onto the tacky surface one-by-one, and let dry.*

# Wheat and Barley Decorative Broom

*Here's a hand-brush so pretty that you won't want to sweep the floor with it. A variation on the traditional broom made from grasses or twigs, this one is made by tying oats and barley together, then adding a bunch of dried lavender and herbs, to give it a decorative feel.*
*Enjoy it even when you're not using it by hanging it by the loop to the kitchen wall.*

## MATERIALS

- bunch of wheat
- small bundle of natural raffia
- bunch of barley
- an assortment of dry herbs and flowers for decoration, such as lavender, sage, mint, marjoram, and a few poppy seedcases
- 20 inches paper ribbon

**1** *Lay the wheat stalks on your work surface, keeping the ears level. Tie the stalks together in bunches of six or eight with a raffia chain stitch. Do the same with the barley bundle.*

**2** *Place the barley on top of the wheat bundle, and tie them together securely with a few strands of raffia. Plait together six 20-inch long raffia strands to make a hanging loop. Tie the loop to the back of the broom near to the top of the handle part.*

**3** *Bind the loop on the handle tightly with raffia. Gather up the dried herbs and lavender, and tie in a bunch; then attach them to the front of the broom with a decorative paper ribbon bow.*

# Herb Tea Boxes

*Before the introduction of tea as we know it today, everyone made their own teas or tisanes from aromatic herbs. Herbal drinks can have healing properties, and are refreshing, relaxing and a general aid to digestion and well-being. The tea is generally made by letting two to three teaspoonfuls of a dried herb infuse in a cup of boiling water for a few minutes. These tea boxes look wonderful in serried ranks on the kitchen shelves.*

## MATERIALS

- plain wooden box
- paintbrush
- acrylic paint
- bunches of dried herbs (see drying project on page 86)

### Properties of herbal teas

*Sage – an excellent tonic and restorative. Helpful in combating stress.*

*Mint – restorative and an aid to digestion. Always refreshing.*

*Rosemary – relieves headaches and stomach upsets.*

*Thyme – relieves coughs and colds, and is calming.*

*Marjoram – aids digestion and calms anxiety.*

*Camomile – a good tonic with digestive qualities.*

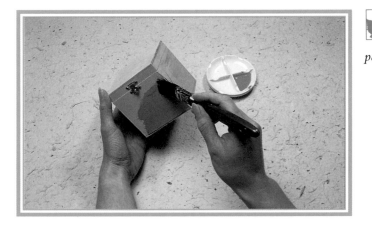

1 *Coat the box with a wash of pale acrylic paint.*

2 *Take a sprig of the dried herb of your choice, this one is mint, and carefully pull the dried leaves from the stems. Fill the box with the dried leaves, and discard the stems. Add a small, hand-painted label to the front of the box.*

# *W*inter

★

Winter's unhurried beauty is seen in the deepest glossiest greens and berry reds set off by a frosted white landscape. And yet, in its stillness, this is the season of hope, as flowers in the purest whites and delicate greens make their appearance. This is a time when people traditionally celebrate, bringing in a small part of nature out of the cold to deck their homes for the holidays.

*a* clear-skied still winter morning offers a peace afforded by no other season. Bare trees, silhouetted against the sky, take on a new elegance when delicately frosted or even cloaked in the heavy mantle of snow. Winter must be the most sculpturesque season: the ordered outlines of pine trees are silhouetted against the sky, and the leaves of evergreens now enjoying the limelight have a stronger, more structured form than those of trees that shed their leaves. This is the season when the various forms of tree seeds are fully matured – exquisitely chiseled pinecones, acorns, and shiny chestnuts.

Against this still background, a few brave flowers poke their heads. Winter pansies, in jewel-bright colors such as azure blue, and golden yellow, bravely make a show despite the weather. Then, later, winter's own flowers appear, just to reassure us that all is not dead. White and the palest greens are the favored colors for the first blooms – snowdrops and hellebores, which include the classic Christmas rose. Now is the time to gather up evergreens and berries, sticks and pinecones, and to turn them into seasonal gifts and decorations. It is also the time to use dried items stored in summer.

## WINTER CELEBRATIONS

The shortest day has been a focus for festivity almost since the beginning of civilization. Yule celebrations, which still give us the Yule log, come from the Viking Juul festival and the seven-day midwinter Roman celebration called Saturnalia – a time when gifts were exchanged. It was the Roman Emperor, Constantine, who, when he was converted to Christianity, suggested that instead of banning the pagan festival, it should be replaced by the Christian celebration, Christmas. New Year's Day in our modern calendar comes a week later, and in many countries this is the time for even greater festivity and merrymaking. The Twelfth Night after Christmas is when the decorations are traditionally taken down. This was the day in pagan times when folk would go wassailing – groups would bang drums and clash cymbals in an attempt to frighten away the evil spirits and insure good fortune for the coming year. They would return to the village to quench their thirst with a warm drink of ale, sherry, roasted fruits, and spices, commonly called and still referred to as the wassail cup.

Many of our traditional customs and decorations predate Christian times, even for this Christian festival. Mistletoe, for example, was a symbol of fertility used in Druid rituals, and even nowadays it is customary to kiss under the mistletoe. Also, in Roman times, evergreens were considered magical because they retained their leaves through the cold winter months, and laurel and bay leaves were used to make celebratory decorations. The Christmas tree came much later – popularly believed to be widely introduced in Britain by Prince Albert from his native Germany in Victoria's reign.

## NATURAL DECORATIONS

In centuries past, all Christmas decorations had to be natural for want of any other material. There is still a sense of satisfaction in making your own – gleaning what you can find from around the house and countryside, and making it into something very beautiful. Natural colors and materials make a pleasing combination on the traditional Christmas tree, and because they have been brought in from the surrounding countryside, invariably look right. There are two sorts of

natural material: evergreen that can be used fresh; and material that is either already preserved, or does not need any preservation. The former includes bare branches and pinecones, dried fruit and flowers, and leaves preserved with glycerol.

## FRESH DECORATION

Fresh material needs to be conditioned so that it will last through the festivities. Fortunately, evergreens not only hold water well, but they're given an added advantage if they're used outside, because the cold means there's less evaporation. Always use pruning shears to cut material outside as a clean cut causes less damage to the tree. As soon as you get home, cut off an extra ½ inch at a sharp angle, so that the branches or twigs can take up as much water as possible. Put them into a bucket of water, and let them soak for at least a couple of hours. Woody branched greenery, such as holly, mistletoe, and fir, will last well, even if it is simply tied in a bunch to be hung up without water. Finer-stemmed greenery, such as ivy does need water, and can be arranged in blocks or rings of floral foam (Styrofoam), which you will need to soak well before using. Inside modern centrally heated houses, most material will need to be in water – either in vases or floral foam. Decorative focal points of fresh flowers can even be incorporated by putting them into preserve jars concealed among the greenery.

## MAKING DOOR WREATHS

The easiest way to make a door wreath is to start with a ring of floral foam (Styrofoam). When it is soaked, cover it with moss, fixing this in position using floral wires – bent hairpin-style. This gives an attractive base for the wreath. Next, add the greenery – holly, ivy, or pine – pushing the stems straight into the foam. Finally, add the decoration – traditional berries, pinecones, bunches of cinnamon sticks, or even cut citrus fruits. If any of these begin to look a little past their best, replace them with new as the holidays progress.

## FASHIONING A GARLAND

Garlands mark celebration in many cultures throughout the world. At Christmas it is customary to drape one over the mantel or twine one down the banister, adding seasonal impact through the house. Traditionally, the base is a piece of thick rope, the length of the finished piece, to which greenery, berries, and decorations are wired. However, it is now also possible to buy very realistic fake pine bases, which are much easier to handle for anyone who is not a professional florist. The base can be supplemented with fresh greenery – a little more pine, perhaps, or holly or ivy to give a completely different look. This should be wired into bunches before being wired to the garland. Finally, colorful decorative touches, such as citrus fruits, berries, fresh or false, cinnamon sticks, pinecones, even terracotta flowerpots filled with goodies can be added. Fresh greenery and central heating aren't generally the best of friends – so try to keep the central heating turned off when the room is not being used. If parts of the garland begin to look a little tired, just replace them.

## USING DRIED MATERIAL

Dried material available through florists, department stores and gift shops has progressed beyond recognition in recent years. Modern hot-air and freeze-drying methods have gone a long way to preserve the colors and even the form of flowers, greenery, seed-cases and fruits. Freeze-dried flowers, though still very expensive, retain a softness, suppleness and much of their original color, so they look almost as if they've just been picked. But even if these are rather more costly than your budget allows, the modern hot-air-dried material provides a lot of scope, too. There's more and more available in both the traditional flowers and in dried fruits – rings of apples, citrus fruits, slices of pears, beautifully showing off their curvy lines, and even completely dried oranges and pomegranates. The spice rack too can be raided to make decorations – silvery bay leaves threaded on wires look fabulous, chilies offer festive hues, and cinnamon sticks, cloves, and star anise provide exquisite texture, color and scent. The beauty of all these materials is that they can be kept and adapted the following year.

As well as decorations, these materials are wonderful for gift-wrapping and cards. It's easy to create impact by perhaps fixing on lines of cinnamon stick, bay leaves, or cloves, or using dried fruit slices.

## THE GOLDEN TOUCH

Even if glitz and glitter is not your style through most of the year, a touch of gold does give any gift or decoration a Christmas feel. Even the simplest materials take on a new dimension with the addition of just a touch. There are several ways of doing this, and each gives a different effect. Gold spray generally gives good cover, lending an all-over gold look, adding opulence to nuts, leaves, pinecones, and spices. You can create a rich gilded effect by completely spraying a whole decoration, such as the holly wreath on page 109, or try a softer look by simply spraying some of the components and leaving the others natural. Gold spray should not be inhaled, so use it in a well-ventilated room, preferably with the window open.

A completely different gold effect can be created using a gilding wax, applied by finger. It lends gold highlights, allowing the natural color and texture of the original material to show through. You can exercise more control with this than with a spray, as you can apply as much or as little as you like. You can create a decoration from the most mundane everyday items.

# Treasure Box

*Make up a nature box to hang on the wall, filling each cubicle with different items. It works best if, as we have done, you aim to group varying textures and sizes. The arrangement can be adapted to incorporate some newly found treasure, or even completely changed with the seasons, offering variety throughout the year. This box is easier to make than it looks. The mitered glass frame is simply a picture frame, and the box itself and compartments are straight pieces glued and lightly pinned together.*

## MATERIALS

- 8 × 10-inch piece of hessian
- 8 × 10-inch piece of plywood for the base
- ⅝ × 1⅜-inch wood 37 inches long for the sides of the box
- small hacksaw
- wood glue
- molding pins
- hammer
- 8 × 10-inch picture frame with glass front
- 30-inch piece of wood for the section dividers
- PVA glue

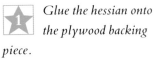 *Glue the hessian onto the plywood backing piece.*

*Saw the 37-inch piece of wood into two 10-inch lengths and two 6¾-inch lengths. Glue and pin the pieces together to make a rectangular frame. Glue and pin the frame to the plywood backing. Cut the narrower piece of wood into lengths that will fit snugly inside the box.*

*Glue the compartment dividers in place. The size of the compartments will depend on the items to go inside. Use smaller lengths of wood to subdivide the compartments farther for tiny objects.*

*Fill the compartments with your own personal treasures, and then glue on the glass-fronted frame.*

# Christmas Decorations

*Raid your store cupboard to make your own Christmas decorations. Dried bay leaves, tiny red hot chilies, twigs, pinecones, and cinnamon sticks are perfect materials. Either string them together on raffia, or thread them onto wire rings, before decorating them with fabric strips and seasonal leaves.*

## MATERIALS

- medium-gauge wire
- pair of sharp scissors
- pliers
- tiny dried chilies
- scraps of gingham fabric
- cinnamon sticks
- pinecones
- dried fruit slices
- dry bay leaves
- raffia
- tiny twigs

 **1** ***To make dried chili rings***, *cut a piece of wire about 8 inches long. Using the pliers, make a tiny loop at one end. Thread the dried chilies onto the wire.*

**2** *Bend the end of the wire through the first loop to complete the ring. Finish off by attaching a fabric hanging loop and bow.*

**★3** ***Make the other decorations*** *by tying up bundles of cinnamon with raffia, then attach a dry bay leaf. Or simply thread bay leaves onto raffia, then tie on tiny twigs.*

# Miniature Pinecone Tree

*Miniature Christmas trees make delightful table decorations. This one, consisting mainly of pinecones, has been given seasonal color with gold-sprayed nuts and red hot chilies. Make one as a centerpiece, or several smaller ones that can be used to adorn each place setting. Dry floral foam forms the basis of the tree. Pinecones are simply wound around with wire and pressed into the foam. Other decorations can be either glued or wired into place.*

## MATERIALS

- tiny red chilies
- medium-gauge floral wire
- pliers
- craft knife
- pinecones
- terracotta flowerpot
- small cube of floral foam for the pot
- sponge
- gold acrylic paint
- whole nutmegs
- dried holly leaves
- 10-inch high cone-shaped floral foam

**1** *Thread three or four tiny red chilies onto a 6-inch length of floral wire. Bend the wire in half, and twist the ends together. Make about 20.*

**2** *Wind a 8-inch piece of floral wire around the base of each pinecone, pushing the wire in between the scales. Leave the ends free to fit into the floral foam.*

**3** *Paint about 10 nutmegs and holly leaves gold. Fill the flowerpot with floral foam, and place the cone-shaped floral foam on top. Fix in place with pieces of U-shaped floral wire. Push the wired pinecones into position, and fill in the spaces with the chilies and holly leaves. Glue on the nutmegs.*

***Finishing the flowerpot***
*To complete the festive, golden look, sponge some of the gold paint onto the flowerpot to create a mottled effect.*

115

# Decorated Candleholders

*Pinecones, cinnamon sticks, driftwood, and pomanders make evocative natural candleholders that perfectly complement the color of beeswax. And with both candles and holders decorated with cloves and star anise, they impart a spicy aroma to scent the room.*

## MATERIALS

- sheets of natural beeswax
  - craft knife
  - ruler
  - candlewick
  - metal skewer
- cloves, cinnamon sticks, and star anise
  - large oranges
  - marker pen
  - small squares of aluminum foil
- power drill fitted with a flat wood bit
  - piece of driftwood
  - small basket
  - dry floral foam
- assorted dried greenery such as pinecones and leaves

**1** *Cut the beeswax sheet to size: a rectangle for straight candles and a triangle for the tapered ones. Lay out the wax rectangle on your work surface. Cut a piece of wick about 1¼ inches longer than the short side of the wax sheet. Place the wick at the end of the sheet, and curl the edge of the beeswax around it.*

**2** *Continue to roll up the candle around the wick. The beeswax will stick to itself.*

*Pierce the surface of the candle with a metal skewer to make rows of small holes spiralling around the candle. Push a whole clove into each hole. Star anise pods and cinnamon sticks can also be pressed into the soft surface of the wax.*

**4** ***For the orange base*** *cut a hole in the center at the top of an orange, just large enough to hold a small candle. Mark guidelines on the skin with a marker pen. Use a skewer to make small holes along these, and push a whole clove into each one. Wrap a square of aluminum foil around the base of each candle, and insert into the top of the orange.*

***Driftwood candle holder and dry arrangement***
*Using a power drill fitted with a flat wood bit, drill a shallow hole in the surface of the wood, just large enough for the candle to fit snugly inside. Make sure that the piece of wood will lie flat, and not tip over when the candle is lit. Fill the base of a small basket with dry floral foam. Cut a hole in the center for the candle. Surround the candle with a dry floral arrangement or pinecones.*

# Corn Picture

*Sheaves of corn make wonderful decorations – and they work best when gathered into bunches. Here, they have been bunched onto a board and tied around with raffia – always a marvellous complementary material for corn.*

## MATERIALS

- 9 × 6-inch piece of fiberboard
- 18 × 13½-inch piece of hessian
- pins
- sewing needle
- matching sewing thread
- power drill
- sheaf of corn
- pair of sharp scissors
- bodkin
- raffia

 *Lay the fiberboard onto the hessian. Wrap the hessian around the fiberboard, and pin neatly in place. Stitch the raw edges together with a large herringbone stitch and matching sewing thread. This will be the reverse side of the picture.*

*Using the power drill, make about six holes through the fiberboard about halfway down. Trim the corn to size, and gather together in little bundles. Thread the bodkin with a strand of raffia, and stitch each bundle to the fiberboard, taking the raffia through the holes to the back and then to the front again.*

**3** *Finish off by threading a few strands of raffia from the back through the end holes to the front. Tie the raffia in a bow. Make a 6-inch long braid from raffia, and fix to the back of the picture to form a hanging loop.*

# Mulled Wine Sachets

*What can be more evocative of Christmas than the rich, warm aroma of
mulled wine. Make up sachets of spices, bouquet garni-style, to flavor red
wine, and pack them into cloth bags trimmed with nutmegs to give as gifts
throughout the whole party season.*

## MATERIALS

- spice mix: 4 cinnamon
  sticks, dried peel of
  1 lemon, 3 whole grated
  nutmegs, 24 whole cloves
  and 1 teaspoon ground
  ginger
- pair of sharp scissors
- 4¾-inch square of
  cheesecloth for each sachet
- 10 × 6-inch rectangle of
  gingham
- colored embroidery
  thread
- sewing needles and pins
- pencil
- 14 × 2-inch strip of
  gingham
- matching sewing thread
- safety pin

**1** *Place a spoonful of the
spice mix on the
cheesecloth square, and fold the
square in half diagonally.
Using colored embroidery
thread, stitch the sachet
together in a semicircular line.
You can mark the semicircle
with a pencil line as a guide.*

**2** *Pull up the running
stitch to gather the
sachet together. Secure the
thread with a few small
stitches, and tie the ends
together in a tiny bow.*

*Fold the gingham rectangle in half, matching the short ends. Stitch the sides together about ⅝ inch from the raw edge. Turn a narrow hem along the raw edge of the opening, and then turn a ⅝-inch hem to form a casing. Stitch close to the fold with matching sewing thread.*

**The spice mix**
*Break the cinnamon sticks into small fragments, and place in a bowl. Add the other ingredients and mix well. This quantity makes about 12 sachets.*

**4** *Turn the bag to the right side. Fold the long strip of gingham in half lengthwise, and stitch around the raw edge, leaving a small gap in the stitching. Turn the strip to the right side, and slip stitch over the gap. Unpick the seam at one side of the casing, and thread the gingham drawstring through, using a*

*safety pin. Drill a hole through two whole nutmegs, and tie onto the gingham drawstring. Fill the bag with the spice sachets, and tie the drawstring in a bow.*

# Fragrant Flowerpots

*Preserved flowers and scented leaves make a traditionally popular winter decoration. These pretty arrangements contain dried larkspur, lavender, and poppy seedcases, together with fragrant herbs such as sage, thyme, and marjoram. Essential oils can be added to the arrangement if, after a time, the natural scents begin to fade. Arrange them in groups in tiny terracotta flowerpots for a look that will not date.*

MATERIALS

- small terracotta flowerpots
- dry floral foam
- knife
- pair of sharp scissors
- assorted dried flowers and herbs, lavender, pink larkspur, sage, marjoram, thyme, poppy seedcases and leaves, and dried bay leaves
- power drill
- 1 whole nutmeg for each flowerpot
- ball of string

**1** *Use a knife to cut the floral foam to fit the flowerpot, and press inside. Trim the stems of the dried flowers and beginning at the center of the pot, push the stems firmly into the foam. Work outward in concentric bands. Finish the arrangement with a row of poppy seedcases or clusters of dried bay leaves.*

**2** *Drill a hole through each of the nutmegs, and thread with a piece of string about 20 inches long. Thread the nutmeg halfway onto the string, and tie the string in a knot to secure the nutmeg. Tie the string around the flowerpot twice, and finish with a double knot.*

# Natural Christmas Cards
# and Gift Tags

*Let nature decorate your Christmas cards and gift tags. Collect dried fruit slices, spices, leaves, and seeds, then arrange them on assorted papers. The simpler designs, in which spices are lined up in rows or circling around dried fruits, are often the most successful. Use your imagination to create a multitude of different designs.*

MATERIALS

- assorted papers such as handmade or those with texture
- pair of sharp scissors
- double-sided sticky tape
- quick-drying craft glue
- whole cloves, tiny chilies, sycamore keys, dried fruit slices, star anise, cinnamon bark, and dried bay leaves
- paper punch
- ball of string

**1** *Cut a rectangle of paper about 9½ × 6 inches. Score down the center, and fold in half. Take a smaller rectangle of contrasting paper, and fix it to the front using double-sided sticky tape. Use handmade paper that has a deckle edge (see page 29), or tear the edge carefully for the same effect.*

**2** *Use a quick-drying craft glue to fix the fruits and spice pieces to the front of the card.*

**3** *Make a gift tag* in a *similar way but with smaller pieces of paper. Cut a rectangle of paper about 9½ × 6 inches. Punch a small hole in one corner, and add a string to fix the tag to a package.*

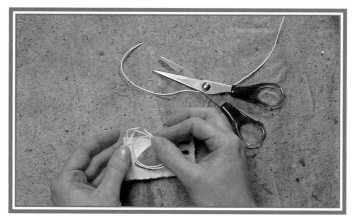

# *i*ndex